a metaphorical god

Also by Kimberly Johnson

Leviathan with a Hook

For Brenna —
Don't stop turning over the pages,
ploughing through the books . . .
— Kim

a metaphorical god

poems   kimberly johnson

KBerryh

KCC Oct 09

A KAREN & MICHAEL BRAZILLER BOOK
PERSEA BOOKS / NEW YORK

Persea Books, Inc.
853 Broadway
New York, NY 10003

Printed in the U.S.A.
Designed by Bookrest.
First edition.

Library of Congress Cataloging-in-Publication Data

Johnson, Kimberly, 1971-
    A metaphorical god : poems / Kimberly Johnson. -- 1st ed.
        p. cm.
    "A Karen & Michael Braziller Book."
    ISBN 978-0-89255-342-6 (original trade pbk. : alk. paper)
    I. Title.

PS3610.O36M48 2008
811'.6--dc22

2008004194

ACKNOWLEDGMENTS

Grateful recognition is due to the following publications, in which
some of these poems, occasionally in different form, first appeared:

*Black Ridge Review, The Chariton Review, CutBank , Harvard
Review, Hotel Amerika, The Iowa Review, Isotope, The Journal,
Meridian, Michigan Quarterly Review, The National Poetry
Review, New England Review, New Orleans Review, Prairie
Schooner, Saw Palm, Slate, Sonora Review, The Southern Review,
32 Poems, Western Humanities Review, Xantippe, Yale Review*

I am profoundly grateful to Michael Greenfield, who endured the
writing of this book. Thanks to Gabe Fried and all at Persea Books
for enthusiasm and support. I am indebted to those friends who
responded to earlier drafts of poems in this collection. Special
thanks to Jay Hopler, my truest ear.

This book was completed with the generous support of a Creative
Writing Fellowship from the National Endowment for the Arts.

NATIONAL
ENDOWMENT
FOR THE ARTS

Contents

My *God*, my *God*, Thou art a *direct God*, may I not say a *literall God*, a *God* that wouldest bee understood *literally*, and according to the *plaine sense* of all that thou saiest? But thou art also (*Lord*, I intend it to thy *glory*, and let no *profane misinterpreter* abuse it to thy *diminution*), thou art a figurative, a *metaphoricall God too*; A *God* in whose words there is such a height of *figures*, such *voyages*, such *peregrinations* to fetch remote and precious *metaphors*, such *extensions*, such *spreadings*, such *Curtaines* of *Allegories*, such *third Heavens* of *Hyperboles*, so *harmonious eloquutions*, so *retired* and so *reserved expressions*, so *commanding persuasions*, so *persuading commandments*, such *sinewes* even in thy *milke*, and such *things* in thy *words*, as all *prophane Authors*, seeme of the seed of the *Serpent*, that *creepes*, thou art the *Dove*, that flies.

John Donne, Expostulation 19
Devotions upon Emergent Occasions

inveni longe me esse a te in regione dissimilitudinis.

Augustine, *The Confessions* 7.10

1.

Epilogue

Before the sackbut, before the virginal
struck perpendicular chords, our madrigals
were sublime, loosing harmonies

to unhinge the spheres. In chantries unrehearsed
we'd wow the votarists and serenade
the friary to panting ecstasies,

while summoned to kingly chambers we branked
the troubadours, turning the sovereign mind
to heaven, the courtiers left speechless

with neglect. This turvied world our work: glib
as conjurors, as priests at consecration,
we scorned the staff-nets, the sinuous crutch

of clefs, that the voice unfettered might raise
grander *magnificats*. And we suffered
no attending scribes, who with sly quills

might bootleg our impromptus, make them fast
and dead, our ingenious antiphons
abstracted on an inkstained palm. It's the piss-

and-vinegar flesh gives music form,
the limber tongue, the wet throat. Keep your small-change
fame, minstrel accolades.— Give us

the measure of the irrecoverable
hour, that miraculous tragedy:
a little tomb, but flashy while it lasts.

2.

Ash Garden

Spring begins in a fatness of front lawns,
but not mine. I whose blowtorch urge approaches
the ascetic, whose resolve to bury

luxuriance grows raw-handed from shoveling,
have duly torched and shoveled grass until
the baked blades crumpled like old palm fronds

and their upturned roots drooped. Let spring begin
in ash and dust, I say, and bloom as little
as possible out of them. I'm planting

stonecrop, and rockmat, and if the fireweed
insists on sowing itself in cinders
I'll truckle it to my lenten aesthetic

or pluck it out: I'll parch the ground six weeks
to prompt by thirst the fireweed's fancy,
gratuitous pink to put on the drab.

Let it learn in sackcloth colors to thrive
on desire alone. It's a discipline
I'm ripe to teach. I excel at fasting.

Opening the Word

Our text today is the heliotrope
swiveling its holy troupe, a charming fence

above umbrage tangled where leaves intergrown
are intercoursing in fat succulence
and each bunch threads down an orgy of roots,

blind mazes to imbosk the sense. Let us
lean not to our own blear understanding
standing under such lovely thrall, but squeeze shut

the hoodwinking eye. The world's plain voice
scrapes and grumbles its burden, stripped
as early spring, sure as the hoar lying

over the violet bed, and so forthright
we take it for honesty. O brothels
and cisterns, my tongue is a fovent choir,

a cloven fire. Listen if your ears be true.

A Psalm

1.

First the high pitch of blood inside the ear
then another high sound inside the first,
a vibrato caterwaul from that stunned

and blurry infant face. Such blank noise.
So nonplussing that foreign tongue, that most
foreign body, open-mouthed and trembling,

baltered with my unfamiliar blood.
Its slippery weight perplexes my arms.
Estranged below the spinal block, my womb

spasms as the mouth finds a breast, the room's
sudden hush a gasping for the next word.
                    —Forgotten the lullabyes

and nursery rhymes, and not yet learnt
our idiom of two, the private
grammar of gestures that will be our vulgate,

2.

I begin to sing the alphabet.
It sounds like disarticulated prayer.

On Divination

Why does the haruspex eye the entrails? Why
mutters the dog pacing the porch, the red sun
eclipsed to a filament in the sky's belly?

The ouija board jolts and will not spell.
Perseids. Leonids. Red skies at morning.
Two-headed calf. Blood in the well.

Even the tea leaves look bad. They slosh
at me balefully, stick against the cup
a flat khaki message in capital letters

—could I but read. Am I to read
this spatulamantic squiggle as next week's
crash? This playing card as coming plague?

What a maddening, a metaphorical
God you are, all frills and periwigs
when plainclothes would do. Flutter

not these fruitless billets-doux
before me: I would far
prefer to face my fate unfreighted

by the parlor game of prophecy. Or
give it to me straight,— lest my predictable
blindsiding blame not poor oracle me

but your coquetry.

Love Song

Stay, adder, startled from the spikenard
by my step. Adder, stay—, lissome syrinx,
temptress of my underbrush. Slither not

so swiftly, though in slithering you dazzle,
scales scintillant under noon. Under noon
I sought you in these grasses, dazzled

by your splendor even deep in grasses,
with my pencils sharpened into points of green
and green. How sharp the emerald pencil,

and the sharper chartreuse, to chart
the deadly pattern of your skin—
that sleek defiant pattern wreathing knots

concentric as you writhe, or is it
dark striations pulling taut? Your skin
so seeming simple is in motion complicated.

When I master its motions, I'll sew myself
a dress of emerald and chartreuse, thin chemise
with knotting wreathes to dozy contemplation.

Then watch me work the garden. Down
among grasses and spikenard my whiplash
glance, my sidewound sashay, who

will resist? What power's in desire:
with admirers seeking, chasing, charting...
Nothing on earth could make me stay.

A Psalm of Ascents

1.

Rank and damp the vapors, backstaggering
out the greenhouse door for stricter soils
I set out, to instruct my looser soul

in the postures of piety. Forty
desert days should scorch my concupiscent
senses to meekness, swerve devotion

from this fond flesh, this riveting
shambles, toward some legible heaven.

2. Death Valley

The basin's rim absorbs with its basalt
the predawn gray. Heartbroken have I hastened
to this heartbroken place, most humble earth

knuckled beneath the reach of water, hot
as hell and godforsaken. Knuckling I
kneel into the gravel and brace for day.

3.

Sunrise in adagio, vastly pink
over the Hundred-Year Bloom, the sand waste
flush with primroses,
                          blown anemones,

verbena blaring in gold and purple,
scrolls of fiddleneck, a fallen sky
of golden aster
                    sticky aster
                                  false

star
        star lily
                    Bethlehem lily.
Even the joshua's spikes are spiffed
with lilies.

4.

    Fuzzed with pollen, fat bees

nuzzle the desert's unaccustomed
frillery, nectared legs slick and swagging.
Outlandish busybodies, so far

from their apiary comforts, they stroke
the orchid's perverse opulence and fidget
the gravel in clusters, the dewy ground

beaded in sticky, waggling gold.

5.

With strange throats the cardinals gloat
over their luck *what-cheer-cheer-cheer*, their cheer
drooping in doppler retreat as they swoop

from me, ever from me further, red flight
into a field of color. I am caught
red-handed— no, red-*hearted* in flagrant

delight. My knees confess it, unbending
up from the razor gravel all bloodied
with primroses.

On Divination by Filaments

This is my body, this broken jumble
of fingernails on my tongue, sharp at the edge
where with dogged teeth I gnaw them off.

So easy-pieced, this thin humanity?
So *insignificant*? Ten cuticles
fretted into orts, a confusion

of cut hairs on the salon linoleum,
the cells I dust behind me as I walk,
all unregarded. If I were holy,

I could believe my body accidental,
a mere adjective of soul, and trouble not
for its disintegration. But removed

so far from holy I take my sloughings hard,
as if each dropped particle were shot
with all my substance, a patchwork sacrifice,

an offering to plead me: *I die daily.*

Ode on Lanugo

From the Latin for *fleece*.
And I was fleeced of mine ages ago,
before I could protest. If lamblike I came
into the world, spindly in my innocence,
how briefly meek, how quick my hankerings
turned fierce, to greasy chops and shanks. Pity me:
I'm heaven's dupe, nursed to a delicate mouth
but turned out into pastures too wolfish
for milkteeth. My pink skin marks me
conspicuous, I caper like an easy mark,
passive and disarming, my plaintive bleat
catches in the throat, comes out growling.
Lamb of God, we have so much in common.
Come, let us lie down together.

Ode on My Belly Button

My original wound was my deepest:
half-inch divot where the cord shriveled off
and a plunging ache that never scabbed
where my umbilical name sloughed away,—
forgotten now, but it meant *Belong*. Whole
again and joyful when my ninth-month
belly swelled with genial weight, skin taut,
fullest at the center line where fragile
the navel flattened out, its secret flesh
splayed to surface, until my familiar
agony: headlong and vulnerable,
our mutual attachment already
obsolescing, you inherit your original wound.
                —Your original loneliness.

Ode on My Episiotomy

Forget pearls, lace-edged kerchiefs, roomy pleats,—
this is my most matronly adornment:
stitches purling up the middle of me
to shut my seam, the one that jagged gaped
upon my fecund, unspeakable dark,
my indecorum needled together
with torquemadan efficiency.
But O! the dream of the dropped stitch! the loophole
through which that unruly within might thread,
catch with a small snag, pull the fray, unknit
the knots unnoticed, and undoily me.

Don't lock up the parlor yet; such pleasure
in unraveling, I may take up the sharps
and darn myself to ladylike again.

Ode on My Appendix

My old frivolity. How I admired
your gentle defiance in my side, your
droll x-ray like a stuck-out tongue showed
sinews fooled to welcome...what? a tag-end,
embroidery, a thing indifferent.
So I believed. But when you flare up,
puckered heretic, my guts clench, bowels
revolt, breath short: you prove the searing
center of my frail cosmology, my
dearest intimate. I pick wistful
at the scar, each whipstitch tugs two grommets
open in my belly. In the body,
in the body's hot memory, in sickness
and in health, there are no adiaphora.

Ode on My Cancer

Rampant, bloody butterfly, my wayward
thyroid flecked its winglike lobes with tumors,
its antic throb across the sonogram
all loveliness—: a vivid, sylvan show
more terrible than the imagined black
blotch, black canker corroding my tissues,
black crab furtive with scuttering claws.
Not crabbed at all, this lift of wings expanding
to fill the screen, their cathode glow
fills the clinical dark, flutters my skin
in green. My heart flutters in my throat
at this strange creature taking wing
in whose cells I am magnified, lush in heyday.

The Melancholy of Anatomy

One white bucket of hearts, their brown chambers
visible and raw. One bucket of wombs.
One mazed with guts, one heavy with wet lungs,

and one full of hands, like a reception
silent and amiable, tenderly
dissected to show each muscle's posture,

the mechanics of bone and white tendon.
White-coated the anatomist works
scalpel and pick, unbreathing, coaxing

the layers apart: epidermis from
dermis, adipose, translucent fascia.
The anatomist never looks up,

tries never to think on the lab's humane
piecework—not that the scene's too gruesome
but too stately, in its bloodless displays

no remembrance of the messy blessed
animal. To prepare the practical
exam the anatomist pins a suite

of specimens with alphabetic tags,
which arranged on the white table will spell
something mournful, something unutterable.

On Divination by Birds

                    I don't need that black

wind of crows kicking up from flax to tell
heavy weather coming, white days to drop
barricades across the interstate,

against two hundred miles of trackless white.
(The crows so obvious then against the miles
of trackless white!) More tricky the magpies

flicker and croak at the sunken carcass
of a roadkill deer, raveling with beaks
the rubbery guts, picking gravel

from scant meat: there must be in their turn-taking
some pattern, some elegant design
beyond need, something in the raw trouble

of jays, the ragged braying geese flown south.
I gaze at their weightless wingbeats daylong
working to discern whether V might stand

for *valediction*, or *vigilance*, or
the blank indifference of *velocity*.

Bust

Let pass the burnt-out smithy
smocked with rust, let pass the pockmarked
headframe canting at the ore-dump,

let pass the tramway, unmaintained
and vacant long of ore-cars,— still
this town would say *surrender*. I read it

on the houses fronting Main, handframed
mortice tight to tenon, paint thinned
beneath the weather, topaz

to beige, gold to slate, ages empty.
The tractor speaks it standing at half-field,
harrow sunk to hubs in dust, the town

an alloy of town and dust: the rails disused,
the dust-dull houses, the road that switchbacks
to the mine—a fine, dark dust borne topside

in bronchioles of men who, scraping for the lode,
unwitting excavated pressure
and a toxic black despondence.

I feel half-dust myself, dried out and stung
by the sandblast wind, on which a map
of swallows is unfolding. And folding.

Three Bouquets

1.

What awful love worked this superfluity?
My U.S. Geological Survey map
grids the haphazard landscape into restrained

geometries, bulges and sandstone hoodoos
smoothed by the benign cursive of contour lines.
But look!— At the chart's least cluttered corner,

the cartographer abandoned
his strict piety to boutonnière
the desert: a compass rose, its freehand

arabesques transgress the quadrants, a baroque
whimsy of the official pen. I imagine him
gripping silent his staves and theodolite,

stumped by some unmappable beauty, it bucking
his measure, efflorescing in him—.
Heartstruck he tricks out the plateau in posies...

2.

Fond romantic, I've followed the map farther
than asphalt, taken myself up to the bare
coordinates where the compass rose blooms.

I'm quick to see the cartographer's flourish
as a valentine, quicker to want what beauty
forced its mark here, to lose my bearings by it:

let my north be this rosy seduction
of sandstone flashed with quartz, my east that far, high mountain
shining like all the kingdoms of the world.

3.

My dear cartographer, how misplaced our faith
in the compass rose, as if its love-knot
could fix beauty. As if it marked anything

but the heart's excesses. My own heart surges
to pitch its rococo against the map's hard facts.
It is willing to break itself to flower.

Vanity of Vanities

Starlings: *little stars*, I thought, but
not these vermin, thieving dregs
from the dog's bowl, marauding nesting eggs.

And don't be fooled by beauty, wet
the sheen upon the gullet, green
the light beneath black feathers. I've been

out back with a BB gun for hours
holding off their thrusts and stares,
bald hollowboned shenanigans

to reach a clutch of unfledged larks.
My routine altered: now up at dawn
to ward against an early attack,

now skipping lunch, crouched on the porch,
I shoo these trash birds all afternoon.
I'm addled, vexed. I yowl and flail. I lurch

the yard to discover their hideout,
my maddening, blackeyed adversary,
my many-winged foe who in phalanges routs

despite calculations my canniest strategy.
For still on the lawn their black constellation
bides unhurried until, spent, I go in.

They'll eat the larks, which I have never seen,
and cannot know, and do not own.

Georgics of the Mind

No almanac forecast this cold snap: cracked
pipes, oak buds shocked to black, the paddocked colt
caught without his winter coat. I tack burlap

to the casement, take in the calf (orphaned
fluke, his dewlap stiff with cold) and scrap
my book-wisdom. To everything there is

no reliable season: the stars
lie, the birds migrate with an animal
disregard, the moon has harlot moods,

all the indices of good husbandry
pure claptrap. We rough mechanicals
ought have our own logic, a calendar

innate, a barometric rise and fall
of blood. Such time spent grappling hand to furrow,
such seasons breeding the flocks to strength

must have gained me fluency in the windfall
without warning, in the volunteer stalk,
the prodigy, the latent trait expressed,

the postscript evidence of things not seen.
How prostrate now the frostbit tilth reproves
my eyes and ears: it knows the studious tract

thrives with spring confidence until sudden
winter brittles it into supplication.

On Divination by Knuckle-bones

It never feels like risk. Brash with glamour,
sequined and overperfumed, the crush
at the craps table shrieks at each loose

of the dice. Two hot breaths into the palm
and then I shoot. I yearn toward their fall,
we all yearn that way, breathless to see

what comes up, what ivory grace paid out,
what jackpot jangles with the assurance
of getting lucky. We tense beneath

our sparkle, betting on a hard-way proof
of open-handed providence. Outside,
the Strip sparkles, the strip-joints and chapels,

the casinos, the temple on the hill,
the city with all its brilliant lights burning
to catch the auspicious eye of heaven.

The Story of My Calamities

Misit ad nos epistolas et totam scripturam,
quibus nobis faceret amandi desiderium.
—Augustine

O God my God, would you were an Abelard
bowing each long midnight in your close cell
over paper, quilling so fervent strokes
to tear the page *My sister, my spouse.*
Would you brooded on the wide between us
unmanned with love, and in a florid hand
hatched assignations, which I in secret
bosomed up, panting for the hour. Constant
then and sure I'd be, as heaven-centered
as an astrolabe. But I can't fathom
your love-letters: libertine troth to the
second-person plural, dry *agápe,*
and all your woo is *Touch me not.* My Lord my flesh
your tablet make.   Inscribe *desire* in me.

Exercises in Translation

For me the broad wallop of swans just airborne
means your exorbitance, forlorn as I was
by both beside the lake: wings above me
too far to reach, and you beyond belief,
idiotically aloof. I tried
my arms around you, tried *against* with thinnest
membranes, even tried *inside* as far as fit,
but always the metaphysical
poverty of a preposition. Pity
my ancient folly, learnt from the Greek,
where longing that presses improvidently
into perfect strangeness takes the name
of *Leda*. Alack! the more I grasp at you
the more I want your beautiful remainder.

Love-letter

Yours is the face scarcely imagined. Yours
the voice that seduces never heard,
yours the throat that frames my gardened
paradise. Yours the rake and yours
the windrows, yours the wind sweeps through
to blast me. Yours the fretless neck
of my desire, the fretful knock of my desire's
echo. Yours the secret junco in my breast:
nights it beats me open, flutters east
to greet you rising with its shrill aubade.
Traitor bird, to wing the windrows
wormed with dawn and yet return
to hole up in my hollows nothing fed, no
song but that unanswered *yours yours yours*.

A Lodge in a Garden of Cucumbers

Isaiah 1.8

1.

What spectacular mulch we hauled!
Under the gloaming the opaline midden
sheened the pales. Blame the climate's heavy
exhalations for sultry grass, beetles sultry
in their mucus, weeds of exotic
variety, and at the end of all
our labors an engorgement
of cucumbers. They swell at dawn,
slick in cucumiform splendor, plump
bunches stretch long into furrows,
oodles in wanton vines—: brave greens,
bold greens, cocksure blossoms.
Hours we doubled over rows, weeks
coddling seedlings for this bonanza.

2.

But what rude hands will pluck,
what barbarous chops devour
these our first, our only fruits
now you have deserted?
Already shutters hang skewampous.
The roof won't hold the rain. Windows
faced with plywood, door nailed shut,
everything nailed shut, and chickenwire
can't keep out the vines, vines
that tendril through each crack. Can I behold
my drear retreat, my sweet regret? My Love,
when you sup with your coterie
gloze not about your garden: call it *the big con*.
Nor reminisce your lodge: Faithless, call me *chump*.

Than longen folk to goon on pilgrimages

Prayed loud all night and so humbled over
I'm hoarse, with a slight stiff neck, but muzzled
you unforthcome. April's a bad season
for silence, what with the ice buckling, buds
cracking to leaf, vines liquored up and flush
under the shower's suit. Lush spring sirens—
my courage pricked more, to speak bold,
by those fool melodies in the oleaster
with no peep from you. Like wind the whirlwind
sounds, the many waters plash and gurgle,
and in what hallows ever seeking, I
hear only in granite echo my own
voice: heated, punch-drunk, broken with longing.
What blissful martyrdom desertion is.

On Divination by Fire

Or rather, the turnings of fire: *first sea*
and of sea, half is earth, half firewind—
Heraclitus knew fire's a showy number,

near-burlesque in colored scarves, turning
firewood to ash and heat. One hot Mojave
day, summer wind blasting from the east,

I watched a dust-devil muster, twist
taller and taller in slow revolutions,
all yellow glitz in the spotlight sun,

the turning shaft and tassels gone to fire
beyond that paltry stage, those cheap effects
of lighting, now turned some pillared sign, bare

transfiguration. But I'm an easy room.

Sweet Incendiary

In this hot light, the seraphim

might look like anything: juniper
flounced in wind, flashing spoil
of jasper, the dove that flies,

anything with a little
shimmer to it, and some
allegorical precedent.

O for an obvious angel,
face of flame and flaming wings,
and golden dart enflamed to thrust

my breast and thrusting pierce again,
my breast like honey melting
with delicious wounds. Or rather leave

these Golden-age extremities:
give me a shotgun angel
to shuck me in the back

of his chariot and break
for the state line, shack up, rip
the veil and show me the shining

undeniable face of God.
No such luck. No glorious
gristle for my fancies

but what I bring myself.— See
my jerry-built epiphany?
Car battery wired to my tongue

set to switch-on my own shimmer,
the spark like a burning coal,
like honey for sweetness

as I mouth the hallmark motto
of heatstruck martyrs: *Lord*
let me suffer or let me die.

Babel

My God, it's loud down here, so loud the air
is rattled. Who with the hissing of trees,
the insect chatter, can fix devotion

on holy things, the electrical bugs
so loud the air is stunned, windy the leaves'
applause redoubled by the clapping wings

of magpies? Who with a whispered psalm
can outvoice their huckster cackle, the trees
blustered to howls while the tesla bees

whine loudly to the shocked air? O who
can think of heaven in such squall, shrill wind
of trees, magpie wings and throats in fracas,

the bluebottle static, the air stupid
with the shrieks of devils,— of angels,—
who in such squall can think of anything

but heaven?

A Closer Walk with Thee

1.

This hairshirt starts to chafe, my Lord, these heats
the death of me. Wide sunburnt wilds with locusts
shrieking in the locust tree. Thank God

for honey: balm my tongue, honey
locusts down the throat. When will you weary
of me your faithful blank? When will I see to *see*?

2.

This heatshirt starts to burn, the sun to wild
the locusts from their tree. My faithless balm,
my God, I chafe my throat with shrieking,

try to tongue the name of honey. Try to tongue
your holy blank, but I weary. O when
will this wide dark, this death drop down?

3.

This chafe's become my balm, its deathless
heat a holy tongue. Tongue
me, honey,— I burn to wear your fires,

to dark the sun with burning, to blank
locution at the throat. When I see
thee in me my eye (*my Lord!*) starts to burn—

Aubade

Got shut of that shitbox, gunshot
splintering to matchsticks Boom-
Age plywood, feeble joists.
Thirty-three west basin days, and I
am sick to death of this campshack,
its ceilinged sleep coins me
claustrophobe. Cloister me
with cirrus, noctilucent, sluicing
west to east past sunset. After dawn
on the skewbald hillside, sagecock
in the rockpile eyes me, puffs up,
retreats and retreats as on the first day.
O desert, desert, my very dirt
parches for you.

On Divination by Wind

My *Complete Meteorology* falls
open to the glossary, where tongue-tied
I've returned to linger on the lavish

particularity of *petrichor*,
name for the smell of long-dry rocks under rain.
Improbable word!— but libraried up

I swear I can smell it, green and vivid
as nectar, as if it sighed from the book
open across my lap. The chapped soul sighs,

opens to knowing like stomata
to southerlies, runs unbodied beyond
my reading hour, beyond the library,

to the moment I push the door open
and step out into the imminent weather,
the pressure's plummet, the fresh gale

tossing palm trees in slangy hosannas,
all in expectation for the first drops
to release that astonishing perfume

whose name I savor, a canonization
improbable as blood from a stone.

Jubilee

No seduction in the hothouse, its aisles
of deliberate orchids heave only
beneath ceiling fans. The horticulturist's
a bawd: her monstrous offspring affront
with chromatic perfection, charm in array.

But when the orange orchard blossoms,
I am ravished.

Raptures in the garden? Never once did rows
of carrot so well-weeded yield
a swoon. *Damn that flim-flam man,
the farmer*, I flare from the fenceline, *sowing
season by season an almanac theology.*

But when orange blossoms wave
in pneumatic arcades, I dither. I coo. I *hallelu*.

The Doctrine of Signatures

Giambattista Porta, sunburned, intent
on the ranunculus, repositions
his sketchpad, headscratches whether the bloom

more resembles a red homunculus
fainting in swoon or a rheumatic fist.
His other sketches show in minute hand

the likenesses of lung to lungwort, the bruise
of color through the iris, the beetroot
swollen like a dropsical foot, the field

spraddled in lovely, grotesque anatomies.
He is careful in his study, careful
painting his pocket apothecary

to let each plant reveal by its sure signs
what it will cure. He loves the body so—
not with a charnel curiosity,

not like louche bone thieves and hair-sellers
but with the relic seeker's pious greed,
or like Solomon smitten, who sang

Sheba into gardened fame: *Thine eyes, love,*
are as the fishpools in Heshbon, thy breasts
the grape-clustered vine, thy nose like apples.

Queenly woman, she must have smiled to read
herself disfigured by his praise, all that
wisdom for a miscellany: sheepflock teeth,

armored neck and a honeycomb tongue,
immortal and unrecognizable,—
inly wishing he'd just learn her favorite flower,

remember every dress she ever wore.
But as she posed swooning in his arms
like limber meadowsweet, she sensed how love

seeks to remedy its shortfalls with compares,
how the body makes monsters of us all.

Marking the Lambs

As crickets geiger-up for spring, we corral
the ram lambs. They stutter and dense against the fence,
wheezing for the ewes. Down wince,
down retch: up one and flip his back to mud,
knee to sternum. The banded tail will black
to wizen, prune off easy. But marking is all trespass:
thumb the soft belly to pop the scrotum out, then lunge and turn
the mind away, teeth working, working, to snap back
and spit. I try not to taste but I am
all mouth, all salt blood and lanolin. I hear
their bleatings through my tongue. They call it *marking*
for the tooth-scars on the belly, but when I speak
tonight, my words will sputter and decay, and when try
to say your name I will pronounce it *elegy*.

Ortolan

If with your serviette you cover not your eyes,
if gluttonous you swallow hot, if fail
to pop the liquored lungs and heart,

with what dishonor will you lunch, how loutish
you'll be labeled. Belly to the ritual!—
we've had such pains to lay it out, to land

such eminent amenities: plum company,
linens broidered with spun gold, the sterling
silver chafing dishes of a toe's breadth.

Our pâtissier's superb, but our charcuterie's
divine. Our chef's beside himself
those stark pink carcasses in hand. He claims

a high fire seals the herbfields of Provence
in crackling skin, a figgy flavor lingers
from Morocco in the musculature. A mouthful host

to leagues, a moment fatted by long months. This
is our illicit joy, this flutter of a whole life
on the tongue, this mysterious taste

of sky inviolate,— this is our craving:
not their tiny innocence defiled, but we
for eating utterly transformed.

Goodfriday

It is true: the thunderhead hoists its wet anvil aloft.
Swifts buckshot out before the downdraft.
The basin gasps, sage exhales, smelling of iron.

Westbound, the hightop two-lane wavers
under early-season heat, asphalt takes
the thinnest shine, first drops hiss.

My truck blows a white wake through roadside
weeds, radio snaps electrically. It is true.
But it is a horror. It is a viper fanged, this verb

that forward thrusts the moment eternal, nails
each thing to its present. Truer still
I should write *the thunderhead converges, lifts, rides*

the steep low, butts the front range, bunches like shoved
fabric, blisters, throws up lightning thirteen miles,
lets down rain in ribs, bubbles under the afternoon...

An endless poem of thunder. But who can dwell
with thunder? The moment's span
would whelm the longest page, its magnitude

of too much weight for me. (*The leader forks, drops,*
attracts the charge from earthward, the molten air
expands, chills, slams shut, a riot of electrons...)

But God, I love the verb. I verb impenitent,
luxuriant, altaring up truth for immortality, for
the pleasure of unlikeness, the prick

of unlikeness! O happy deformation,
spunky verb, I embrace you in my
degradation, my shoddy embodiment

making thunder endless: impossible: sublime.

[   ].

Through weather. Through weather's declensions.
Through spring's steep degrees, through five shapes of snow,
through the thunderhead's sexual green

over green geometrical acreage,
through every stormy declension
of the heart I have cried your name. It is

a histrionic's litany, recited
from this, my usual station: *Unrequited*.
Where else such sighs and bluster, such tropics

of squalling passion?

*

               And what is wind
but a dialect of longing?—: the high
pressure rushing to fill the low, the sky

trying to slake its heats against the earth's
asymptotic cool, its somersaulting cools
against the earth's radiance. All weather

springs from currents of failed desire. No wonder
the wind, when it says anything at all,
howls.

*

O fugitive God, my glorious jilt,

my heart has learned a tempest's grammar
in your pursuit. Listen: it thunders up
its truest, its most hopeless, prayers

for you.

Easter, Looking Westward

1.

The stars! the stars have fled the sky!—
Scratch that— the stars have *skyed the flood*, the sea
glimmering in pale beneath a starless black...

2.

No, scratch that too. I'm all exotic
metaphor, inkhorn snarls, never content
with the unelaborated *thing*;

always the forced apotheosis,
every least sparrow a visible sign,
strong-arming water to wine. So tenderly

I love this world's profane loveliness,
its small, scarce loveliness, like a puritan
I batter magnitude out of homespun.

3.

Faithless my zeal, for the puritan's faith
imputes us all with a roughhouse grace, most
lovely in our brokenness, bruised and bent

to glory.   Scratch that— to sufficiency.
Start again: The stars are black with storms
blown shoreward; the dinoflagellates

smacked on the shoals leak light from shattered cells;
they phosphoresce the breakers in their roister.
Let me sing, then, the beauty of creatures

microscopic, who make the vastness gleam
in smithereens.

4.

                    See: starlike, after all.

3.

Voluptuary

Fifty-mile Creek in the extravagance
of June, a fullness of flowers: paintbrush
and larkspur, beeflower and attendant bees,

the cedars *sough*, the sunfired pines
forge filigree at the timberline.
My ballerina sister on the riverbank

balances, rod cocked to rearward,
released, and retracted, line tripped
terpsichorean by the weight of the fly.

Her tacklebox cockeyed reveals homemade
damsels: the Emerging Sparkle, the Orange
Sunrise, the Dark Scintillator, and a Green

Butt Skunk. A ridiculous scene, tableau past
cliché, with verdure and soughing
and blah blah blah. She hooks a splake,

flips him to shore, yanks her knife open,
swipes anus to jaw. With a finger inside
she slides guts, gore, and shit in a shining

red pile. She dunks him, lets the stream
clean the gash, chucks him to me
for the icebucket, and here the suckerpunch

of beauty: white vault of ribs in their arch
to the spine, one red vein bulging faithfully
skull to tail, red gills fragile, useless

beneath the operculum, ordered
like layers of vellum. Scales flake off
and stick to my palms like glitter.   Like silver.

"Opening the Word": This poem owes its life to Donald M. Friedman's splendid essay "*Comus* and the Truth of the Ear." With gratitude and affection.

"Ode on My Appendix": In the period following the religious Reformation of the sixteenth century, there were many doctrinal issues for which their devout defenders were willing to go to the stake. But there were also questions which were considered to be, relatively speaking, theologically unimportant; these matters were described as "adiaphora": literally, *things indifferent.*

"Georgics of the Mind" takes its title from Francis Bacon's 1605 treatise *The Advancement of Learning*, and was written for my fellow-laborer Kevis Goodman.

"The Story of My Calamities" is the title of Abelard's autobiography. The epigraph, from Augustine's commentary on Psalm 64, reads: "God sends the whole of scripture to us as a love-letter, by which to provoke in us a longing to love him."

"Sweet Incendiary": The italicized plea with which the poem concludes is Teresa of Ávila's.

"The Doctrine of Signatures": Renaissance polymath Giambattista della Porta promoted this natural philosophy, which held that the pharmacological virtues of plants could be interpreted by their visible characteristics. See especially his *Phytognomonica* (1608).

M